The Life and Music of Elvis Presley

Biography for Children
Children's Musical Biographies

BABY PROFESSOR

EDUCATION KIDS

Speedy Publishing LLC
40 E. Main St. #1156
Newark, DE 19711
www.speedypublishing.com

Elvis Presley was one of the greatest singers and musicians to come out of the American South. Let's find out about his life and his music!

Early life

Elvis Presley was born in Mississippi in 1935. He was one of a pair of twins, but his brother died at birth. Elvis was devoted to his mother. They lived in a mixed-race, church-going community and Elvis' later music reflects rural, African-American and church-music influences.

Elvis first sang in public, standing on a chair to reach the microphone and dressed as a cowboy, at an agricultural show when he was ten. He got his first guitar soon after that, although at the time he said he would have preferred a bike or a rifle.

He learned guitar slowly at first and then had lessons from relatives and from the pastor of his church. At the time he would play in public but was too shy to sing. Classmates at school thought of him as a poor hillbilly. But when he was 12, Elvis performed on the radio for the first time on a program hosted by Mississippi Slim, a musician Elvis loved.

When Elvis was 13 the family moved to Memphis, Tennessee. He began studying the guitar more seriously and playing in public with several other friends. By the time he left high school Elvis had determined music would be his future. He was inspired by both the black and white musical scenes in Memphis and started dressing in the style of the performers.

He got over his fear of performing and singing in public. He was becoming a competent guitar player even though he never learned to read music, and he knew popular music of the time very well. He was also an expert in the blues, country music and gospel songs.

Breaking into music

Sun Records was looking for some way to expand its audience for African-American music. Much of the United States was still segregated and it was hard for a black performer to get and hold the attention of the white audience.

Producer Sam Phillips thought that if he could find a white musician who could sing with the drive and energy of African-American singers, he could make millions. Elvis Presley turned out to be that performer.

There were several false starts as both Phillips and Presley kept trying to get Elvis to sing like an existing star, rather than perform naturally. Finally, at the end of a frustrating recording session in 1954, Elvis grabbed a guitar and started singing an old song his way. The studio musicians joined in on a wild jamming session and the resulting record was so popular that local radio stations played it over and over to respond to listener requests.

Elvis began recording and performing more and developing his vocal and visual style. He was so nervous at early concerts that his legs would shake and his wide pants legs emphasized the movement. The audience thought this was new and exciting and Elvis kept the movements long after the nervousness was gone.

By 1955 Elvis Presley was a star in Tennessee and East Texas and appeared regularly on radio. His music had great energy and drive and combined country-music traditions with African-American rhythm and blues in a way audiences had not heard before.

FROM
ELVIS PRESLEY
BOULEVARD,
MEMPHIS,
TENNESSEE

RCA

On the other hand, some radio stations would not play his records because Presley's "rockabilly" style did not fit well into either country or rhythm and blues traditions. At the end of the year, Presley signed a deal with the national record label RCA Victor.

In 1956, Elvis appeared on television for the first time. His new albums, now with national distribution, helped to define and build the audience for the new style of music that came to be called "rock and roll".

His first album was the first rock-and-roll album to hit the top of the charts and it stayed there for ten weeks. With Presley, the guitar took over from the piano as the main and central instrument in popular music.

With television appearances, Elvis' very physical style with hip grinding and suggestive body moves, caused a scandal. What he did was very mild by the standard of music videos today, but in the 1950s it was considered outrageous and not suitable for family viewing.

Of course, for many younger people the fact that their parents were offended by Elvis Presley made him even more attractive to them. Presley seemed to give teens a voice and a style that informed and electrified a whole generation.

Elvis' public concerts became more and more frenzied. You could hardly hear the music or his singing for the screams and applause. Record after record became the number-one seller, not just in the United States, but around the world.

Elvis had ambitions of becoming an actor and released his first movie in 1958. But that same year he was drafted into the army and was away from performing for more than two years. He served in a tank unit in Germany and was a good soldier, but at this time he started using amphetimine drugs. He thought they were great for strength-building and weight loss and had no idea of how addictve they were, or how much harm they could do to a body.

A decade of movies

When his military service was done Elvis re-started his music career along with making a series of movies. He wanted to be a serious actor but after a couple of attempts at "real" movies with serious story lines had only modest success, he mostly stuck with what came to be called "soundtrack movies".

The movies were tightly-scripted boy-meets-girl stories, with little ambition and lots of opportunities for Elvis to sing. Then the soundtrack of the movie would appear in stores as the movie appeared in theaters. The plan was a financial success, but the movie-related music became less and less inventive and less and less interesting to the audience beyond Presley's fanatical fans.

Back to live music

In 1968, Elvis moved back toward playing and singing the music he wanted to do, in the way he wanted to do it. With a television special and a series of hit records, he basically re-started his career. He released hit after hit, ranging from hard rock to ballads to unusual Christmas music to an album of gospel tunes and toured widely.

He was a music phenomenon. However he also moved away from his musical roots into the broad middle ground of music acceptable to the white, mainstream listening audience. He began wearing extreme, remarkable costumes that in many way, set the tone for what singers wear now in music videos.

An extravagant life

Elvis married Priscilla in 1967 and they divorced in 1973. His health was going downhill partly from the pace of his working life and partly because of his overuse of prescription drugs.

Elvis had a fear of becoming an alcoholic as many of his family members had been, but somehow convinced himself that any pill he got through a doctor's prescription would be okay to take. He became addicted to painkillers and other pharmaceuticals and gained a lot of weight. He was suffering from liver damage, high blood pressure and many other ailments.

Elvis had always enjoyed a public image that combined a sexy "bad boy" with a man devoted to his mother. As the 70s wore on, he became more and more a symbol of extravagance. His home in Memphis, Graceland, was a huge mansion full of staff members and hangers-on who were living off him.

He drove extravagant cars, like his three pink Cadillacs and wore costumes covered in rhinestones and other sparkly jewels. Finally Elvis Presley's body could not support the strain he put on it. He died in 1977, at the age of 42.

The impact of Elvis

Elvis Presley changed the way young Americans of his generation saw themselves and the way the nation and the whole world listened and danced to music. He combined religious, ethnic and regional musical traditions in new ways. He was so popular that more than a dozen Presley recordings, released after his death, became top-ten hits.

Some African Americans resented Elvis, feeling that he had stolen the fame and success that black musicians should have had. During his life, Elvis repeatedly pointed to the African American performers and composers as his masters and as the people deserving real fame.

Graceland, the Presley home, gets over half a million visitors each year. The only residence that is more visited in the United States is the White House, the president's home in Washington, DC.

Honoring Elvis

If you like Elvis Presley why not learn some of his songs? You don't have to wear a white body suit or have a fancy hairdo, just sing the song and have as much fun doing it your way as Elvis did doing it his way. Then look through other Baby Professor books to find what you can learn about other musicians and other types of music.

Made in the USA
Columbia, SC
21 February 2018